Contents

The Hunt Begins 1
Peregrine Falcon 6
Dhole 10
Saltwater Crocodile 14
Snow Leopard 18
Great Barracuda 22
Assassin Fly 26
Bull Shark 30
Yellow-throated Marten 34
Osprey 38
Western Ghats King Cobra 42
Spot Them Here! 46
Fact Finder and Credits 47

The Hunt Begins

Every animal has its place in the food chain – a special order in nature that shows "who eats who". The food chain starts with tiny plants and grasses on land and phytoplankton and algae (the tiniest of aquatic organisms) in water, which are eaten by herbivores (plant-eating animals). These herbivores, from the graceful antelope to the cute little squirrel, become food for the next group – predators.

Why Do Some Animals Hunt While Others Eat Plants?

Predators are the hunters of the animal kingdom and are carnivores (meat-eating animals). They simply can't digest plants properly. Their stomachs and teeth are designed to break down meat, not leaves. Habitat (the place where they live) also plays a big part. Wolves, tigers and other carnivores can't munch on grass. But their habitats have animals that they can hunt. And they've developed abilities to make the most of it!

Bull sharks are found in the seas surrounding India

How Do Predators Hunt?

Hunting is essential to a predator's survival, and they have all sorts of tricks up their sleeves – from chasing down deer to ambushing prey from the shadows. The mighty eagle uses its amazing vision to spot prey from astounding heights and snatches up its meal with razor-sharp talons. Meanwhile, a crocodile snaps up fish or large animals that wander too close to the water's edge with its powerful jaws.

A snow leopard found in regions of the Himalayas

Hunting with the Pack or Going Solo

While some predators prefer to hunt alone, others like to hunt in packs with their buddies. The dholes use their numbers and wits to nab prey, taking turns to chase and corner their target. On the other hand, tigers, leopards and many other apex predators (animals at the top of the food chain) are lone hunters. These animals rely on their stealth and strength to bring down their prey without any help.

Escape Artists: Surviving a Predator Attack

So what does the prey do? Animals lower in the food chain do their best to avoid becoming a tasty meal. They have special skills – speed and defensive tactics – that give them a fighting chance against their hunters. The dance of predator versus prey is a deadly game. While we feel sorry for the prey that ends up in the tummy of a tiger, it's hard not to admire the skill of these predators. Get ready to meet them!

Agumbe in Karnataka is home to a large number of king cobras

Peregrine Falcon

Find Me Here!
Look for hunting falcons around tall buildings, especially near open areas. Pylons along roads are a favourite perch too!

CRITTER STATS
Scientific name: *Falco peregrinus*
Size: 36–58 cm – about the same as a crow
Weight: 0.90–1.5 kg
Lifespan: 13–25 years
Habitat: cliffs, grasslands and even your city!
Conservation status: least concern

The fastest flying bird in the world is also one of India's top predators. When it dives in pursuit of prey, the peregrine falcon can reach speeds of 320 km/h! It is so fast that the prey – usually other birds – may never even see it coming!

Watching a peregrine hunt is a thrilling experience! It can spot its prey even as it circles hundreds of metres above in the sky.

That's like you standing on top of the tallest building in India (an apartment block in Mumbai that's 320 m high) and being able to spot your handkerchief on the ground!

Once it has the prey in sight, the peregrine folds in its wings close to its body and takes the shape of a teardrop. This reduces drag and lets it fly at super speed!

It then plunges down at a steep angle before striking the target with its powerful talons mid-air. **WHAM!** It is death on impact for the helpless prey.

It likes to eat the freshly caught meal on a high perch, but may also snack on the wing!

DID YOU KNOW?

In-built sunnies: the peregrine falcon has a see-through layer of skin that it pulls over its eyes to protect it from wind and dust at top speeds!

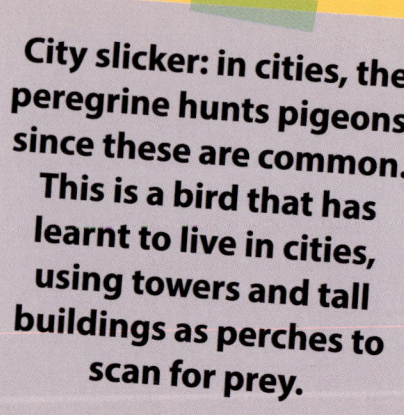

City slicker: in cities, the peregrine hunts pigeons, since these are common. This is a bird that has learnt to live in cities, using towers and tall buildings as perches to scan for prey.

Dhole

Find Me Here!

Once found all over India, you are now more likely to see dholes in the Western Ghats of Karnataka.

CRITTER STATS

Scientific name: *Cuon alpinus*
Size: 90 cm – slightly bigger than an indie dog
Weight: 17–21 kg
Lifespan: 16 years in captivity
Habitat: central and southern India
Conservation status: endangered

Also known as Indian wild dogs, the dholes are pack hunters that prey on species like the spotted deer, sambhar and wild boar. They may also snack on the occasional beetle or bird. These highly social animals work in teams and can bring down animals larger than them.

A dhole pack in action is much like your favourite football team!

There is a plot devised with cunning, and a clear plan laid out for each member of the hunting pack.

Dhole have been known to hunt in groups of 30, though more often, hunting packs may be much smaller – less than 10 dholes.

During the hunt, some pack members lie in wait while the rest drive the prey towards them. This is called ambush hunting. Each hunting pack has a leader, and a chosen hunter gets first grab at the prey.

Dholes are even smart enough to drive fast runners like deer into water. They then swim into the pond and surround the victim. It doesn't stand a chance!

After a successful hunt, dholes follow certain rules – pups get to eat first. Packs even post a member to look out so that the hard-won meal doesn't get stolen by a tiger.

# DID YOU KNOW?

No bark, only bite! This is a dog that doesn't bark. Instead, dholes talk to each other using whistles and other sounds including whines, mews, squeaks, screams, growls and chatter calls.

One for the road – dholes can keep quite a lot of meat in their tummies. They can barf out this food on demand and feed it to their pups.

Saltwater Crocodile

Find Me Here!
Bhitarkanika National Park in Odisha and the Andaman and Nicobar Islands are real croc hotspots.

CRITTER STATS
Scientific name: *Crocodylus porosus*
Size: 3–7 m – half the width of a basketball court
Weight: 1,000–1,200 kg – as heavy as a small car!
Lifespan: 30–50 years
Habitat: India's east coast and islands
Conservation status: lower risk–least concern

Saltwater crocodiles or 'salties' may look like slow, slumbering beasts, but they are the master predators of salty marshes (wet areas) and coastal rivers. Males can grow to 7 m in length – that's half the length of your school bus!

They lurk just beneath the water's surface near the riverbank and wait for prey.

With their eyes, ears and nose right on top of their heads, salties can stay underwater while keeping a sharp lookout for lunch.

Salties float so still that they are mistaken for logs of wood by their prey. Once an animal is close enough, they explode from the water and **SNAP**!

The victim is trapped between two strong jaws, and then it is quick death by drowning. Their powerful jaws can even crush the skull of a buffalo.

This is the animal most likely to eat a human – next time you visit a zoo do not lean into their pen (in fact, that's good advice for all crocs)!

DID YOU KNOW?

Like other reptiles, saltwater crocodiles can grow all their lives!

They are super aggressive, which is why you might see some salties missing limbs – clearly these don't play nice. In fact, they may also make a snack of their own kind.

"Lolong" the Philippine saltie was the biggest measured at 6.17 m and 1075 kg. He died in 2013 and is now on display at Manila's National Museum.

Snow Leopard

Find Me Here!
You can spot them in Ladakh and the Spiti region of Himachal Pradesh. They are easier to spot in the winter.

CRITTER STATS
Scientific name: *Panthera uncia*
Size: 1–1.3 m – like a large German shepherd
Tail length: 0.80–1 m
Lifespan: 18–21 years in captivity
Habitat: high mountains of the Himalaya
Conservation status: vulnerable

The 'ghost of the mountains' is a stealthy predator that uses several weapons in its kit to track and hunt prey. Its greyish fur with beautiful black markings (also called rosettes) allows the snow leopard to blend with the steep, rocky mountains it calls home.

This big cat uses the cover of cliffs and rocks to stalk wild sheep and goats, such as the bharal, argali, ibex and markhor. A powerful body and excellent balance (thank that long tail) help.

With short forelimbs and long hind limbs, this cat can leap a distance six times the length of its body – a true long jump champ!

Snow leopards are expert acrobats and will throw themselves down cliffs to pounce on prey.

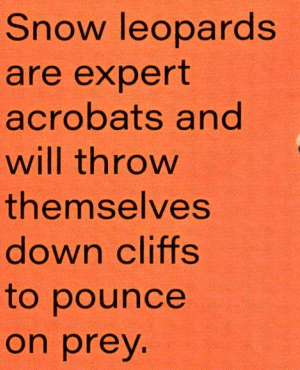

They hunt by themselves and make a kill every 8–10 days, but this big cat has never been known to bring down a human.

 DID YOU KNOW?

They may be called snow leopards, but this cat is more closely related to the tiger.

Large paws act like snowshoes, spreading the weight out so that the leopard doesn't sink into the snow.

Snow leopards are true super heroes of the snow, capable of bringing down prey three times their own weight.

Great Barracuda

Find Me Here!

Diving in the Andamans could bring you face to face with a great barracuda in India.

CRITTER STATS

Scientific name: *Sphyraena barracuda*
Size: 1–2 m – about the same length as a sari!
Weight: 40 kg
Lifespan: 14 years in captivity
Habitat: ocean waters off India's coast
Conservation status: least concern

You may remember the barracuda as the villain who eats Nemo's mom in *Finding Nemo*. Well, this ambush predator of the ocean can also be found closer home, in the Indian Ocean, where it lives in shallow coastal waters around coral reefs.

Great barracudas are extremely efficient predators. Shaped like sleek tubes, they can swim at over 50 km per hour!

When they catch a glint of a silvery fin or scale — a sign that tasty prey may be around — off they go, zooming through the blue water.

Their mouth is lined with sharp teeth, some angled backwards to keep a grip on prey, even fish as large as themselves.

Stealthy great barracudas use their bluish scales to hide in plain sight. Before anyone can yell "Surprise!", they zoom in and snap up the prey fish.

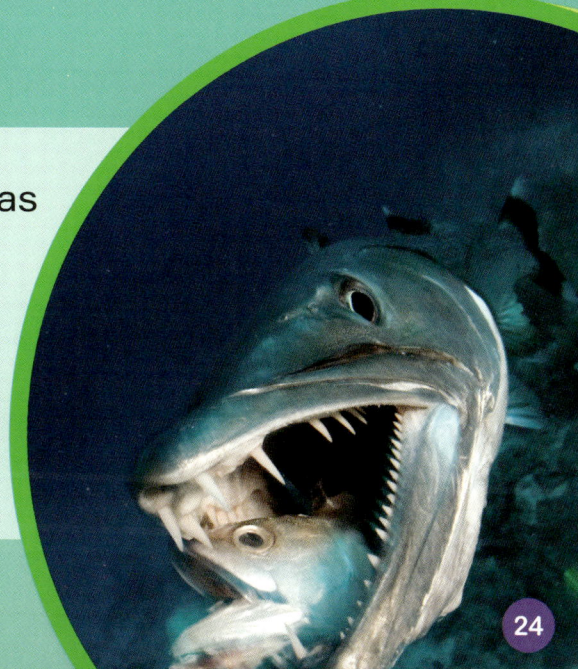

DID YOU KNOW?

As large as they are, great barracudas are in turn prey for sharks, killer whales and dolphins.

Some great barracudas can grow as long as 2 m!

Assassin Flies

Find Me Here!
Although found across India, rainforests such as those in the Western Ghats are an assassin fly's favourite!

CRITTER STATS
Family: *Asilidae*
Size: 9–15 mm – as small as a paper clip!
Weight: just a few milligrams to 2 g
Lifespan: 6–10 months
Habitat: rainforests, under rocks and leaf litter
Conservation status: least concern

This is one deadly fly – the James Bond of the insect world. Assassin flies can take out just about any other insect. Victims include bees, wasps, spiders and other flies. Today, there are more than 7,000 species of assassin flies all over the world, including India.

All assassin flies follow a simple plan. They sit around, perched on rocks and plants, waiting patiently for a victim to come their way.

Once they have locked their sights on their next meal, these predators attack the victim mid-flight and grab it using their legs.

They then take a bite – not because they are hungry – but to inject poisonous saliva (the stuff you spit out). It's death by spit for the captured insect, which is carried away.

Assassin bugs are not picky eaters – they even go after insects larger than themselves if they feel they have a chance to bring it down.

DID YOU KNOW?

Assassin flies don't chomp down their food. The saliva that the fly injects turns the victim's insides to liquid, which it slurps up.

This assassin sports a moustache! These stiff hairs on its face probably protect the bug from its struggling prey.

Bull Shark

Find Me Here!

Bull sharks can also be found in many India's rivers, such as the Ganges and Brahmaputra.

CRITTER STATS

Scientific name: *Carcharhinus leucas*
Size: 1.8–2.4 m – that's as long as a motorbike
Weight: 95–111 kg
Lifespan: 13–32 years
Habitat: rivers and waters off India's coast
Conservation status: near threatened

These sharks will eat almost anything – not for nothing are they one of the super predators of the ocean. While they like to eat fish, the occasional dolphin or turtle also makes for fine food. Bull sharks even prey on other sharks and they hunt by day and night. Clearly a super predator of the sea!

Sharks usually keep their insides salty but bull sharks live in both salty oceans and fresh water.

Since they can handle both 'sweet and salt', bull sharks thrive in estuaries where rivers meet the sea and fresh and salty water mix.

The muddy water of estuaries offers these predators a huge advantage. Prey have a hard time seeing them coming. It helps that bull sharks, like most other sharks, have a super sense of smell.

Their hunting technique is called 'bump and bite.' They bump up against an animal to check what the prey could be before going on to take a bite.

They can keep 'bumping and biting' until the victim is too tired to escape. If you are diving and get bumped by a bull shark, you are in trouble!

 DID YOU KNOW?

Female bull sharks are larger than males . That's because they live longer and keep growing throughout their lives.

Bull sharks usually prey on smaller fish but can also take on larger animals. They have been known to attack hippos in Africa!

To escape their own predators, they vomit out food. The predator is left confused while the bull shark makes a quick getaway.

Yellow-throated Marten

Find Me Here!

Spot a yellow-throated marten on a Himalayan trail, in states such as Uttarakhand and Arunachal Pradesh.

CRITTER STATS

Scientific name: *Martes flavigula*
Length: 50–71.9 cm – like a cat or a beagle
Weight: 1.2–5.7 kg
Lifespan: 16 years in captivity
Habitat: found across the Himalayas
Conservation status: least concern

Cute they look, cuddly they are not. Yellow-throated martens of the Himalaya are fearless predators that few animals are willing to take on. They've even been known to pick fights with eagles and chase monkeys! This predator is right on top of its food chain.

They'll eat almost anything — snakes, rats, lizards, birds, chicken, deer — bring it on! In China, they even prey on panda cubs.

Martens are powerful and can move very fast. Though they usually hunt on the ground, they are good climbers and can scamper up a tree to catch birds.

Some of that fearlessness comes from the trick martens have up their sleeve, or rather up their bottoms. When in danger, they release a stinky liquid from their poop holes, which is enough to put off anyone!

These animals hunt in groups to increase the chances of cornering prey. They are also known to hunt at night around areas where humans live.

DID YOU KNOW?

Yellow-throated martens help out too. These animals eat fruit and poop out the seeds in many parts of the forest, helping new trees spring up.

If they are that fierce, can any animal prey on martens? Yes, but only if the predator is pretty large – think Siberian tigers and Asian black bears.

Osprey

Find Me Here!
Look for ospreys hovering over wetlands and near rivers in the winter, between November and March.

CRITTER STATS
Scientific name: *Pandion haliaetus*
Length: 55–58 cm – about the size of a goose
Weight: 1.2–2 kg
Lifespan: 25 years
Habitat: across India
Conservation status: least concern

There is something fishy about this one – perhaps because almost all they eat is fish. Ospreys visit India's wetlands in winter, and it's quite a sight to see one hunt. One moment it's circling above the water, and the next, it's hovering over a spot (like a helicopter) before diving straight down.

It goes in feet-first to nab a fish with its talons, eyes locked firmly on what's moving in the water. Powerful wings are put to good use to lift off from the water with the fish captured in its sharp claws.

Ospreys can see prey moving below the surface. They are top hunters, catching fish on at least one out of four dives!

They have an oily waterproof coating on their wings so that they don't get weighed down by wet feathers when taking off from the water.

Once the victim is nabbed, ospreys are able to hold on to the most slippery of fish thanks to claws on the pads of their feet.

 DID YOU KNOW?

Ospreys can shut their nostrils when underwater.

Ospreys mostly pair up for life, and pairs may return to the same nest year after year.

When ospreys nab a fish, they turn it so the head points forward. This reduces friction from wind and makes the catch easier to carry.

Ospreys migrate south to warm places like India in winter. During its lifetime, an osprey may clock more than 250,000 migration miles!

Western Ghats King Cobra

Find Me Here!
This shy snake is a rare sight but can be seen in Agumbe, Karnataka – the king cobra capital of India.

CRITTER STATS
Scientific name: *Ophiophagus kaalinga*
Length: 3–4 m – that's longer than a car!
Weight: 4–10 kg
Lifespan: 17 years in captivity
Habitat: forests, swamps and grasslands
Conservation status: vulnerable

Who hasn't heard of the king cobra? This snake is known both for its fighting ability and sheer courage – rare qualities for a snake. But it won't show either until it feels threatened. In fact, a rather shy snake, it likes to keep far away from humans.

The king cobra feeds only on other snakes, though a monitor lizard or small mammals (like rats) may also make for a tasty meal for variety.

What makes the king cobra's venom a killing tool is the quantity – around 7 ml in a single bite. That's enough to kill 20 people or even an elephant.

When threatened, a king cobra can become quite aggressive. It expands its ribs and muscles of the neck to form a hood.

It can also lift a third of its body to stand erect. This, and the spread hood, make the snake look larger, scaring away predators.

 DID YOU KNOW?

The king cobra is the only snake that builds a nest for its eggs.

The king cobra is the world's longest venomous snake. It can become as long as 5.4 m – and grows throughout its lifetime.

It has a hiss that sounds a bit like a dog's growl.

Spot Them Here!

Follow the pug marks to find some of the best places to spot India's amazing wildlife. Creatures such as the peregrine falcon, osprey and assassin fly live across many regions and can be spotted quite close to home too!

Fact Finder

Krishnan, Raghu. "The Peregrine Falcon Finds a Home in High-Rises." *The Hindu*, 24 Mar. 2023.

"Peregrine Falcon." *The Peregrine Fund*, https://peregrinefund.org/explore-raptors-species.

"Dholes: The Fearless Communal Pack Hunters." *RoundGlass Sustain*, https://roundglasssustain.com/species.

Hoffmann, Michael, et al. *Canids: Foxes, Wolves, Jackals, and Dogs – Status Survey and Conservation Action Plan*. IUCN, 2004.

"Saltwater Crocodile." *National Geographic*, https://www.nationalgeographic.com/animals/reptiles/facts/saltwater-crocodile.

"Saltwater Crocodile." *Wildlife Institute of India*, https://wii.gov.in/nmcg/priority-species/reptiles/salt-water-crocodile.

"Saltwater Crocodile Facts and Information." *Animal Spot*, https://www.animalspot.net/saltwater-crocodile.html.

"Snow Leopards." *WWF UK*, https://www.wwf.org.uk/learn/fascinating-facts/snow-leopards.

"Snow Leopard Facts." *Snow Leopard Trust*, https://snowleopard.org/snow-leopard-facts/.

"Great Barracuda." *Oceana*, https://oceana.org/marine-life/great-barracuda/.

"Great Barracuda." *RoundGlass Sustain*, https://roundglasssustain.com/species/great-barracuda.

"Killer Insect Profile: Assassin Fly." *Smithsonian Institution*, https://www.si.edu/stories/killer-insect-profile-assassin-fly.

Ambrose, Dunston P. "A Checklist of Indian Assassin Bugs (Insecta: Hemiptera: Reduviidae) with Taxonomic Status, Distribution and Diagnostic Morphological Characteristics." *ResearchGate*.

"Creature Feature: Bull Shark." *Shark Trust*, https://www.sharktrust.org/blog/creature-feature-bull-shark.

Choudhury, A. "Himalayan Yellow-throated Marten (Martes flavigula) in West Bengal, India." *ResearchGate*.

"What Is the Yellow-Throated Marten? Candid Animal Cam Investigates." *Mongabay News*, https://news.mongabay.com/video/what-is-the-yellow-throated-marten-candid-animal-cam-investigates/.

"Osprey." *National Wildlife Federation*, https://www.nwf.org/Educational-Resources/Wildlife-Guide/Birds/Osprey.

"Osprey Overview." *All About Birds*, https://www.allaboutbirds.org/guide/Osprey/overview.

Daniel, J. C. *The Book of Indian Reptiles and Amphibians*. Bombay Natural History Society and Oxford University Press, 2002.

Whitaker, Romulus, and Ashok Captain. *Snakes of India: The Field Guide*. Draco Books, 2004.

Credits

Picture Credits

iStockphoto: Yash Darji, 2203824170; Kolbz, 172695099; KenCanning, 1291077829; chameleonseye, 533923648; Aekprachaya Ayuyuen, 1472497894; zbindere, 172129117; t_cherdchay, 1127938532; Holly Cannon, 1144665891; Global_Pics, 516532217; tunart, 470643190; Yann Hubert, 486852408; Rainervon Brandis, 175386741, 170429180, 516682445; stammphoto, 611636882; yod67, 814183762; Luc Pouliot, 1327323055; Steve Hinczynski, 1482624105; atese, 1970938876; s1murg, 453404101; ISpi-Photography, 186673282; Thipwan, 1025834850; Aschen, 1308648652; Sanif Mia, 1605736891; Harry Collins, 966715974.

Wikimedia Commons: Dhole (Asiatic Wild Dog) by Anindya007; Cuon_alpinus_alpinus_sitting by Johan Spaedtke; Dhole_Bandipur by UdauKiran28; Dhole_kiss by Kandukuru Nagarjun; Dhole_feeding_Khao_Yai_NP by Tontan Travel; Dhole by Anagha Devi; The_look_of_Dhole by Vinoth Chandar; Saltwater_Crocodile_(Crocodylus_porosus) by Moheen Reeyad; Saltie-eats-fish by Lee Kee Yap; Saltwater_Crocodile_(Crocodylus_porosus) by Nils; Lolong by Julan Shirwod Nueva; Snow_leopard_by_Nicolas-Goulet; Uncia_uncia_2 by Bernard Landgraf; Snow_Leopard_Uncia_uncia by Greg Townsend; Snow Leopard portrait by Tambako The Jaguar; Robber_fly_02546 by Vengolis.

Independent contributors: Peregrine falcon images by Amita Sharma; male king cobra images by Romulus Whitaker; king cobra images by Dhritiman Mukherjee; male king cobras in combat by Steve Alter.

First published by Juggernaut Books 2025

Text copyright © Juggernaut Books 2025

10 9 8 7 6 5 4 3 2 1

P-ISBN: 9789353458188
E-ISBN: 9789353458256

All rights reserved. No part of this publication may be reproduced, transmitted, or stored in a retrieval system in any form or by any means without the written permission of the publisher.

Printed at Nutech Print Services - India